POGO:

PRISONER OF LOVE

BY WALT KELLY

Simon and Schuster • New York

First printing

SBN 671-20401-7
Library of Congress Catalog Card Number: 71-95589
Manufactured in the United States of America

OTHER BOOKS BY WALT KELLY

BEAU POGO

POSITIVELY POGO

POGO

POGO PEEK-A-BOOK

PREHYSTERICAL POGO

THE POGO SUNDAY BRUNCH

GONE POGO

POGO'S SUNDAY PUNCH

THE POGO PARTY

THE INCOMPLEAT POGO

POGO EXTRA

THE POGO PAPERS

POGO À LA SUNDAE

POGO PUCE STAMP CATALOG

UNCLE POGO SO-SO STORIES

TEN EVER-LOVIN' BLUE-EYED YEARS WITH POGO

DECK US ALL WITH BOSTON CHARLIE

THE POGO STEPMOTHER GOOSE

THE POGO POOP BOOK

POTLUCK POGO

THE POGO SUNDAY BOOK

THE RETURN OF POGO

I GO POGO

INSTANT POGO

THE POGO SUNDAY PARADE

EQUAL TIME FOR POGO

G. O. FIZZICKLE POGO

and SONGS OF THE POGO

POGOMOBILE

In collaboration with Pogo: THE JACK ACID SOCIETY BLACK BOOK

THIS BOOK IS

for ANNA WAGONNY CAMERANO

with love...

Contents

THE GOOD OLD
OLDTIME
NEW START

One of the happy accidents of being a cartoonist is the discovery, practically by chance, that people are dependable and steadfast. We can be relied upon for the gold of comic material which also can pan out to be the fool's gold of tragedy. Despite the fact that we repeat our acts of boobism over and over, we are always surprising and fascinating. There is a kind of hypnotism in watching our wriggling mirror reflections.

In these times, the word "student" or the word "cop" can scarcely be uttered by most except as an epithet. We have had constant revolution since the year One because we like to start anew, our way. Having fouled up one home, we leave our litter behind to write a brave new constitution in a land far off and considerably upwind from the dump.

But now, through lack of space, we have to face each other in the dark and uneasy environs of the familiar. So it occurs to the cartoonist that the easiest war is the one in the home where railing males and females, family bound, can relieve the tedium with the age-old fight of love.

THE TRUEST LIE
IS YOUTH REMEMBERED

14

SOME EARLY THREAT
OF PROMISE

WARPATH TO PEACE

YOU SCARED MY SEE-GAR... Y'MADE ME **SWALLOW** THE SCAPER...

YOU ROUSED MY **PER**-FESSIONAL IRE.

WHEN POGO WAS S'POSE TO BE **PRESIDENT**, *I* WAS GONNA BE THE **SECRETARY OF EDUCATION.**

2-13

YOU ....UH ....**WHAT?**

LEARNED TO **READ**...GOT ALL SET....THEN **NOTHIN'** HAPPENS.

YOU CAN **READ**, WILEY CATT?

YEP...KNOW MOST OF THE LETTERS OF THE ALPHABET ....MY FAVORITE ONE IS "**O**"....IT'S SO KIND OF **ROUND** AN' ALL.

YEP, I WANNA BE **SECRETARY OF EDUCATION** BECAUSE I'D LIKE TO BRING EVERY CHILE UP TO **MY** CULTURAL LEVEL.

ORG.

2-14

HOW COME YOU SAYS "**ORG**"?

YOUR CULTURAL LEVEL CONSISTS OF THE ABILITY TO READ **ONE** LETTER... "**O**"...IS **THAT** GONNA HELP KIDS?

20

DEACON! I AND ALBERT GOT A **GREAT** IDEA!

?

WE'RE GONNA **SEE-CEDE!**

My great great Gran'pa tried it once~~~But Gran'ma caught him at the border with the Sunday collection.

All $1.39½ of it.

OH, WE AIN'T TRYIN' NO **PETTY LARCENARY STUFF**... **WE** ARE STARTIN' A **BRAN' NEW COUNTRY**... RIGHT, ALBERT?

YOU LOST MY **SEE-GAR!**

LIKE THE KID HERE SAYS, IF WE STARTS A NEW COUNTRY, **HE'LL** GET TO BE THE **SECRETARY OF GROUN'HOGGISM** AN' I'LL BE THE **SECRETARY** OF **EDUCATION!**

Din't know that either of you was a expert in them fields!

Why'd you quit school after 13 years?

'CAUSE I WAS STIFF.

GOOD BOY!

2-20

DURIN' MY HALCYONIAN DAYS, WE USETA MAKE THE STUFF DOWN IN THE FURNACE ROOM 'TIL A LEAK DEVELOPED AN' EVERYBODY WAS A DROP-OUT...ACTUAL A BLOW-OUT...

I DON'T MEAN THAT... I WAS STIFF FROM SETTIN'...

HOW DULL...

YEP...MAYBE YOU'VE NOTICED... STUFFIN' YERSELF INTO THEM SECOND GRADE CHAIRS WHEN YOU'RE GOIN' ON TWENTY YEAR OLD KIN BE AWFUL TRYIN'...

What else qualifies you to be Secretary of Education?

CHURCHY TAUGHT ME TO READ.

2-21

I LEARNT HOW TO READ HALF OF POGO'S NAME .... I'M A EXPERT ON THE "O" PART... LISTEN...O, O, O, O, O... GREAT, HUH?

"O" is the same thing as ZERO!

24

THE IMPOSSIBLE POSSIBLED

29

31

3-7

CHAPTER 5

AN ANTHEM OF NOTE (ONE)

AND THEN *I*.... HEY!

SEE! SEE WHAT WE HAVE HERE IN THE DOG? THE NEW SECRETARY OF *PROBLEMS*!

?

3-11

WE HAVE *YOU*, WITH A *FIRM GRASP* OF *NOTHING OR ZERO*, AS SECRETARY OF TREASURY AND/OR EDUCATION....*ALBERT*, WHO CAN'T TALK, *SECRETARY OF STATE* ... .*THEN*... *BEAUREGARD*.

HAR! PUT OL' DOG IN CHARGE OF *PROBLEMS* AND YOU'LL HAVE ONES NOBODY HEARD OF.... HE HAD TO SEND OFF FOR A *CORRESPONDENCE COURSE* ON HOW TO TIE HIS SHOES....

EXACTLY! THE PUBLIC IS TIRED OF *OLD PROBLEMS*.... WE NEED *NEW, VIBRANT, FASCINATING* PROBLEMS.... *BEAUREGARD'S BRAIN* WILL SUPPLY THEM, CORRECT?

HERE'S THE KEY TO OUR WHOLE SCHEME FOR *SECESSION*...

♪

3-15

WE, AS A CABINET, NEED A *PRESIDENT*.

Oh, I was eatin' some
Chop Suey
With a lady in St. Looie,
When I sudden hears
a knockin' at the door!

And that knocker,
he said "Honey,
Roll this Rocker out some
money
Or your Daddy shoots
a baddie to the floor!"

CHAPTER 6

THE SOMNAMBULISTIC MISSILE

JOB GOT ONE DRAWBACK....

THINKIN' UP A *REAL* BRAN' NEW PROBLEM IS A *REAL* PROBLEM.

BEAUREGARD, YOU SAY MOLE WANTS YOU TO BE SECRETARY OF *PROBLEMS*?

YEP...A TOUGH JOB.

3-27

THERE'S THE GUY TO HELP YOU...*CHURCHY*...HE'S A VERTIWOCKLE *EX*-PERT ON PROBLEMS.

BUT *MY* PROBLEM IS *NEW* PROBLEMS... Y'KNOW, *THINKIN'* EM UP.

THEN CHURCHY IS YOUR MAN....TO *HIM*, ALL PROBLEMS IS *NEW*.

Z

41

3-31

CHAPTER 7

BRAIN TRUST BUST

WHAT DO YOU THINK OF THE **OKEFENOKEE** SECEDIN' FROM THE **U.S. AND A.**, SAM?

SECESSION IS **ALWAYS** GOOD....ALL ACCORDIN' TO **WHAT** HUNK TAKES OFF...

I'D SUGGEST WE SECEDE WITH A **DIFFER'NT PATCH** OF GROUND CENTERIN' AROUND OUR **HEART** LAND.

4-7

HEART LAND? *WASHINGTON, D.C.?*

FORT KNOX.

SUPPOSE OUR NEW COUNTRY *DID* MAKE OFF WITH **FORT KNOX**....? ...**FIRST** THINGS BEING FIRST?

FIRST THINGS BEIN' **FIRST?**

4-8

WE WOULDN'T PAY **NO TAXES**....

GRAND!

WE'D FEED THE **STARVING.**

?

46

FIRST WE'D BEAT ALL THE OTHERS TO THE **MOON**.... IT BEING MADE OF **CHEESE**....

WE COULD **THEN** FEED THE STARVING.... ....THEM AS CARES FOR CHEESE....

YEH....FIRST THINGS BEIN' **FIRST**.

HERE'S OLD **OWL**....I BRUNG HIM OVER BECAUSE HE'S GOOD AT ALL THE **OCCULTISM** OF RUNNIN' A COUNTRY.

BULLY!

YEAH, **BULLY**.

4-9.

YEAH, I CAN HELP **FORECAST** STUFF AND MEBBE FIND YOUR LUNCH IF YOU LOSE IT.... Y'KNOW?

Y'KNOW, LIKE IF YOU WANT TO GO TO **WAR** WITH **CHINA**, OR ONE OF THEM, HE'LL TELL YA HOW IT'LL **WORK OUT**....

YEAH....I BURN **PRAYER PAPERS** AN' WATCHES **SPIDERS** AN' BRING OUT THE **FACTS**.

GACK.... I **DUNNO**.... WHAT DO **YOU** THINK, SAM?

WELL, YES.... I THINK WE SHOULD TAKE ADVANTAGE OF **ALL** SUCH MODERN METHODS.

YOU BOYS **GO** TO THE FORT AND **POKE** AROUND.... THEN REPORT BACK.

POKE IT IS!

NOW! **WHICH** FORT DID HE SAY?

UM.... **FORT...UH...** HMM...WELL MM · YEH· UM...

HEIGHDY, BEAUREGARD, HOW'S THE **SECRETARY** OF **PROBLEMS** COMIN'?

GOT A BIG PROBLEM WITH OUR **NEW ANTHEM**...

4-12

"OH, STAND UP AND COUNT YOUR NOSES, OUR LAND'S A BED OF ROSES RIGHT FROM YOUR HEAD TO TOE-SES" ...**NOW WHAT NEXT?**

"OUR DOOR WE NEVER CLOSES...." ...AT LEAST IT **RHYMES**... DON'T **MEAN** MUCH THO!

GREAT! GREAT!

LONG AS IT **RHYMES**... WE CAN MAKE IT **MEAN** SOMETHIN' LATER.

49

A SECRET: SWIFT, SHORT, SWEET, AND DEAD

51

4-17

A MUFFLED MISS MUFFET

54

CHAPTER 10

ERGO EGO

AND WHEN THE **QUISLING** YAPPED ON EVERY SIDE, **WHO** SAID "**YE SHALL NOT PASS!**" **WHO** GAVE HIS **ALL**? **WHO**?

YEAH, **WHO**!

ME! THE NOBLE DOG! MAN'S **BEST FRIEND**! A-LERT, A-WARE! NOW **CAST ASIDE! ABANDONED! GULP!** A PIECE OF **FLOTSAM** AND **JELLY-SAM** (...SNIFF...)

THERE THERE... **BLOW**

SUCH A **SORRY** WAY TO TREAT MAN'S BEST FRIEND... **THROWIN' ALL DOGS OUT OF THE ANTHEM** ...HOO... GULP

YOU JUST REST... I'LL WHOP UP SOMETHIN' TO CALM YOU DOWN.

4-26

WHAT'S WRONG, BEAUREGARD?

I'M **CAST ASIDE!** DOWN-SPURNED BY **HITHER TO BOSOM BUDDIES! MAN'S BEST FRIEND**, IS BEEN CRUELLY GIVE THE **BACK OF THE BRUSH!**

WHO DID THIS TO YOU, **OLD FRIEND**...? I'LL START A **PROGRAM** OF **TEARIN' HIM LIMB FROM LIMB!**

HIM

HIM? HUM! MM... WELL, WHY DON'T WE PUT OFF MY PROGRAM 'TIL AFTER LUNCH?

HERE WE ARE.

CHAPTER 11

ENOUGH IS PLENTY

4-29

4-30

59

5-1

CHAPTER 12

EASY COME, QUEASY GO

64

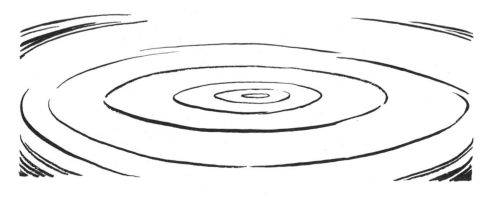

CHAPTER 13

A RANK CASE OF REASON

AN OFFENSIVE **WHAT**?

IT'S AT TIMES LIKE THIS THAT THE **REAL NEED** FOR A B.A.M. SYSTEM COMES **ALIVE**...

5-14

DON'T YOU MEAN THE **A.B.M.** SYSTEM?

NO... I BELIEVE **BAM** SPELLS IT OUT BETTER...

CHAPTER 14

A BUSTLE OF MUSCLE

5-23

DANG! RAN RIGHT INTO SOMEBODY'S NEW WASHED CLOTHES.

5-26

HELLO, SISTER! WERE YOU AT THE BIG LADIES AID RALLY WHERE WE HOOTED AN' HOLLERED AN' CARRIED ON? LANDY LAURA MERCY WHAT A DO!

HEH HEH, THAT SO? WELL, WHAT WAS IT ALL ABOUT, MIZZUS?

OH, LAND! WE SCREECHED AN' SPEECHED AN' WROTE THREATENIN' LETTERS.

MIZ BEAVER GOT IN A THREE ROUND DISCUSSION 'BOUT A MOTION; MIZ RABBIT HAD A SET OF THE SWOONS; WE BROKE 19 PLATES... WODDYA MEAN? WHAT WAS IT ALL ABOUT?

YOU SEEM TO BE HAVIN' TROUBLE WITH YER CLOTHES, SIS.

AIN'T MINE. I RUN INTO 'EM KINDA ACCIDENTAL.

5-27

WELL, I'LL BE.... THIS LOOKS LIKE MIZ BEAVER'S YARD... THAT'S HER WASH, I WARRANT.

ORG

WHEN SHE COMES BACK, I WOON'T WANNA BE IN *YOUR* SKIN, MISS, UH--M-- *WHAT IS* YOUR NAME, HON?

ORG!

ORG? ...STRANGE MONICKER, SIS ....MM, SHORT FOR ORGANDY, I S'POSE .... *HERE* COMES MIZ BEAVER, NOW.

HEIGHDY, MIZ BEAVER, I'D LIKE YOU TO MEET A NEW FRIEND, *MISS ORG.*

OUR LADIES COMMITTEE IS VOTED TO *GIT* TH' *MEN'S PRESIDENT.*

5-28

OL' *MOLE* CLAIM *POGO* IS THEIR HEAD MAN ..... SO, IF WE CAPTURES *HIM*, ONE OF US *MARRIES* THE CRITTUR .....

...THUS BECOMIN' THE *FIRST LADY* AN' THUS GITS TO *RUN THE SHOW!*

WELL, WELL, WELL, THAT MIGHT INTEREST MISS ORG, HERE .... MISS ORG? *HEY, ORG!*

OUT WITH THE WASH

80

6-11

GACKSCRAGGLE EXPLORED

FIRST CLASS,
SPECIAL DELIVERY FEE-MALE

THE EXPERIENCE I'VE HAD WITH A HUSBAND, THE ONE THAT GOT AWAY, PROVES THEY'S INCONSTANT.

THE MINUTE NORMENT GOT OUTTA HAND, I'D GIVE HIM A QUICK RIGHT.... HAD HIM TRAINED GOOD!

BUT HE MUST OF GROWED WEARY OF LOVE....

YES?

HE LEFT ME FOR A SOUTH PAW.

US GIRLS BEEN POOPIN' OUT.... WE SHOULD REMEMBER MY OLD SCHOOL SONG....

Oh, roar a roar for Nora, Nora Alice in the night, For she has seen Aurora Borealis burning bright....

6-17

6-18

6-19

88

CHAPTER 18

THE WONT OF DON'T

90

91

CHAPTER 19

AHEAD IN THE FRIDGE

94

7-3"

7-4

TWO SHOTS FOR THE ROAD

100

OH, I DUNNO, MA'M... YOU GOT **CLOSE**.... LOOK AT THE **HOLES** IN MY HAT.

MAGNIFIQUE! I AM **IMPROVE!** PERHAP NEXT TIME I... ....BUT **NON**....ALORS.... WHAT I AM **SAYING**?

THE **REASON** I AM SHOOT IS BECAUSE OF THE **RASCALS** WHOM ARE STEAL FROM ME SO I WARN THEM **STAY AWAY** OR I **SHOOT** I SAY.....NON?

7-16

WILEY CATT IS STEAL MY RUTABAGAS! I WARN HIM! I LOAD THESE GUN WITH THOSE **ROCK SALTS!** I HEAR NOISE IN NIGHT! I PULL **TRIGGER!**

BUT, UNFORTUNATE, THESE NOISE IS ONLY **YOU**....

GEE... I'M SORRY.

YA MEAN YOU'D KILL A MAN FOR STEALIN' **RUTABAGAS**, MISS?

THE GUN WAS ONLY LOADED WITH **ROCK SALT**.

IT'S **SAFER** TO GET KILLED BY ROCK SALT?

MUCH SAFER.... **COME!** WE HAVE SOME SUPPER.

CHAPTER 21

THE WEIGH OF HER HEART

CHAPTER 22

A REAPPRAISAL OF AGONY

As Secretary of Peace I've come to the conclusion that the conclusion of War will be the conclusion of all.

HUH?

I AGREE WITH POGO.

FORT MUDGE MEMORIAL DUMP

7-29

According to this old Almanac for 1816 we fought our best battle two weeks *after* the War of 1812 was over----

Those people had perseverance---- They understood War was their business----yet they accepted **Peace**----haugh!

HOW COME YOU SAYS **HAUGH**?

What did they accomplish with *Peace?*----Today they're all **dead**----

ALL?

What job does Mole give *me* in this new cabinet? Secretary of Peace----- **Haugh!**

7-30

The new country doesn't want Peace ---- People enjoy **WAR** ---- It's very enlivening!----And whom did Mole appoint as President? **A nothing**----so meaningless that *I* forget who he was----

My first act as President will be to inform my minions that I am President---

A P.R. JOB, PREXY--- LEAVE IT TO ME.

I'll say something simple like --- The finger of fate pokes forth and touches the outstanding man and appoints---

SAY SOMETHING THAT MEANS SOMETHING TO THE **PEOPLE**--- "WE HOLD THESE TRUTHS TO BE SELF-EVIDENT, THAT ALL MEN ARE CREATED EQUAL, THAT..."

A pretty sentiment---but I'd have to have the research team compute that out and verify it---Now where was I?

FORT MUDGE MEMORIAL DUMP

Z

WHAT YOU NEED, DEACON, IS A **QUIT CLAIM DEED** THAT SHOWS YOU NOW OWNS THE JOB OF **PRESIDENT**.

Right.

" THIS CERTIFIES WHEREAS AND TO WIT THAT WHEREFORE I, THE PRESIDENT, HEREBY RESIGN TO BECOME SECRETARY OF PEACE, THEREFORE AFORESAID HITHERTO SEC'Y---

WOOF!

8-5

CHAPTER 23

AN IRREVERSIBLE REVERSE

8-9

CHAPTER 24

THE PRESERVING PERVERSITY
OF PERSEVERANCE

8-13

WAIT A MINUTE... HERE'S **FIREHOSE**: .06 per foot. (complete extinguishment, .07½ per foot)... NICE BARGAIN RATE THERE...

HAW! WHAT **FOR** DO YOU CARRY THE HOSE?

SERGEANT, IS YOUR HOSE **ON FIRE**? ... MMM... **GUESS NOT**... THIS *IS* A PROBLEM.

THAT'S WHAT FOR I CARRY THE HOSE...

BE OF GOOD CHEER, MEN, WE'LL GET THIS FIRE **OUT YET**... NOW THE RATE ON A **TOOL** SHED FIRE IS QUITE NICE...

HEY, CHIEF!

8-27

HERE'S A NICE FIRE EXTINGUISHMENT RATE ON A **POMERANIAN PUP TENT**... THE METHOD ALSO LEAVES A NICE BLAZE BURNIN' ON THE REAR STOOP IN CASE ONE WISHES TO PREPARE **BREAKFAST**...

CHIEF!

WHAT!?

THE **RAIN** PUT THE FIRE OUT.

Y'SEE, BUN RAB... PERSEVERANCE! **PER-SEE-VERANCE**... IT'LL PAY YOU TO CURB YOUR HASTY NATURE.

© 1969 WALT KELLY

119

A REIGN OF RAIN

BY DAWN'S EARLY
AND LATEST LIGHT

125

126

8-30